Clamor

CLEVELAND STATE UNIVERSITY POETRY CENTER
NEW POETRY
Michael Dumanis, Series Editor

John Bradley, *You Don't Know What You Don't Know*
Lily Brown, *Rust or Go Missing*
Elyse Fenton, *Clamor*
Dora Malech, *Say So*
Shane McCrae, *Mule*
Helena Mesa, *Horse Dance Underwater*
Philip Metres, *To See the Earth*
Mathias Svalina, *Destruction Myth*
Allison Titus, *Sum of Every Lost Ship*
Liz Waldner, *Trust*
Allison Benis White, *Self-Portrait with Crayon*

For a complete listing of titles please visit
www.csuohio.edu/poetrycenter

Clamor

poems

Elyse Fenton

Winner of the 2009 Cleveland State University
Poetry Center First Book Prize

CSU Poetry Series
Cleveland State University Poetry Center
Cleveland, Ohio

First edition   5   4   3   2

This book is the winner of the 2009 Cleveland State University
Poetry Center First Book Prize, selected by D. A. Powell, and
is a title in the CSU Poetry Series published by the Cleveland
State University Poetry Center, 2121 Euclid Avenue, Cleveland,
Ohio 44115-2214. www.csuohio.edu/poetrycenter and is
distributed by SPD /Small Press Distribution, Inc.
www.spdbooks.org

Cover image: *Clamor,* by Mary Jo McGonagle. Used with permission.
Clamor was designed and typeset by Amy Freels in Minion.

Library of Congress Cataloging-in-Publication Data
Fenton, Elyse, 1980–
Clamor / Elyse Fenton. — 1st ed.
    p. cm. — (CSU poetry series)
"Winner of the 2009 Cleveland State University Poetry Center First Book Prize."
    ISBN 978-1-880834-89-3 (alk. paper)
    1. Military spouses—Poetry. 2. Iraq War, 2003—Poetry. I. Title. II. Series.

PS3606.E58C57 2010
811'.6—DC22   2009053799

Acknowledgments

Grateful acknowledgment to the editors of the journals where the following poems originally appeared, at times in slightly altered form:

Bat City Review:	"The War Bride Waits"
Best New Poets 2007:	"Gratitude"
Cimarron Review:	"In the Fourth Year of War (Killeen, TX)"
The Massachusetts Review:	"Ballistic"
Natural Bridge:	"After the Blast"
	"Gratitude"
	"Love In Wartime (I)"
	"Notes on Atrocity (Baghdad Air Station)"
	"Planting, Hayhurst Farm"
	"Word From the Front"
Nimrod:	"Clamor"
	"Infidelity"
	"Refusing Beatrice"
	"Your Plane Arrives from Iraq for the Last Time"
Pleiades:	"Aubade, Iraq"
	"The Dreams"
	"Love in Wartime (II)"

Gratitude to Dorianne Laux, Robert Hill Long, Karen Ford, Eliza Rotterman and all the folks at the University of Oregon. To Badgerdog Literary Publishing for the community. To Laurie Capps, Samia Rahimtoola, Lisa Steinman, and Matt Rader for their generous readings and various guidance. To Jericho Brown and D.A. Powell for their insight. To Michael Dumanis, Rita Grabowski, Krysia Orlowski and Cleveland State University Poetry Center for rolling up their sleeves. To Jon Wei, Caroline Morris, Cindy May Murphy, and D.J. Murphy, for their advocacy and distraction. To Marc and Gail Fenton, for their earliest advocacy and insistent support. And to Peenesh Shah, for it all.

for P.—

I want to gather you up
into a book whose pages clink

like bone cockles gaveled smooth
in the blood-wash of unimagined shore—

Contents

II.

III.

clamor—

1. a: A noisy shouting b: A loud continuous noise
2. Insistent public expression (as of support or protest)
3. SILENCE

Gratitude

Wreckage was still smoldering on the airport road
when they delivered the soldier—*beyond recognition,*

seeing God's hands in the medevac's spun rotors—
to the station's gravel landing pad. By the time you arrived

there were already hands fluttering white flags of gauze
against the ruptured scaffolding of ribs, the glistening skull, and no skin

left untended, so you were the one to sink the rubber catheter tube.
When you tell me this over the phone hours later I can hear rotors

scalping the tarmac-gray sky, the burdenless lift of your voice.
And I love you more for holding the last good flesh

of that soldier's cock in your hands, for startling his warm blood
back to life. Listen. I know the way the struck chord begins

to shudder, fierce heat rising into the skin of my own
sensate palms. That moment just before we think

the end will never come and then
the moment when it does.

3

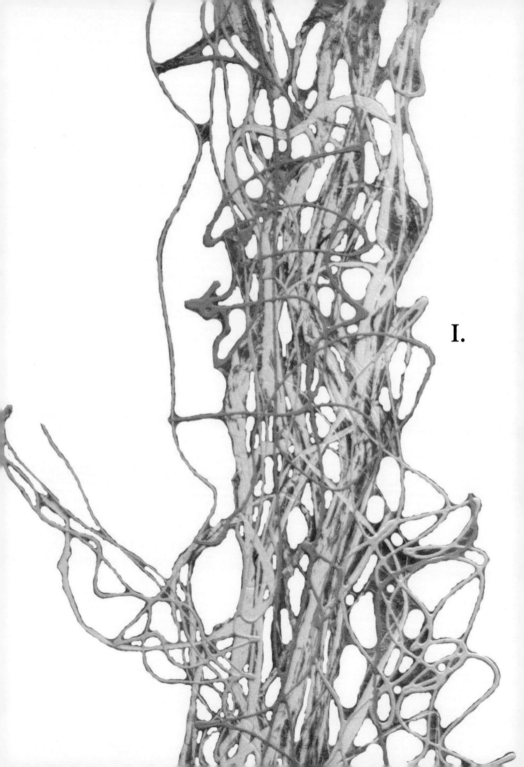

I.

The Beginning

January, Boston. She held his first letter back
from the new front in her hands. Outside, light

and snow clung to the train windows like the paper
edges of a hive crushed in. Later she would remember

otherwise; not the long rows of parking spots
tunneled from snowbanks and marked

with plastic lawn chairs like tombstones
for the unprepared or the pigeons on Comm Ave

mistaking salt for crumbs. Not the neon swarm
of flakes or the first few notes of grief

waiting to unfold. Only that she looked up
from the page—*Only now am I afraid to die*—

to feel the desperate clamor of a train
jerking roughshod through its gears,

the car's slow rocking-in-its-tracks
like the heart's smallest engine

         just beginning to seize—

Love in Wartime (I)

Because there are seven thousand miles
of earth & sky between us. Because

these lines are made of wind & fired
particles. Because at any moment the hard dust
beneath your feet could breach like a cleft
in meaning, could erupt into a sifting
cloud of brick & metal-riven bone

I have to believe in more than *signifiers*—

that the world cannot be dismantled
by the word alone. That language is not
an uncoupling dance or the sparkless grinding
of meaning's worn flint, a caravan of phosphorous
tails burning up the breathable air.

When I say *you* I have to mean
not some signified presence, not
the striking of the same spent tinder

but your mouth & its live wetness, your tongue
& its intimate knowledge of flesh.

Word from the Front

His voice over the wind-strafed line
      drops its familiar tone to answer,
Yes, we did a corkscrew landing down
    into the lit-up city, and I'm nodding

on my end, a little pleased by my own
      insider's knowledge of the way
planes avert danger by spiraling
    deep into the coned center of sky

deemed safe, and I can't help but savor
      the sound of the word—the tracer round
of its pronunciation—and the image—
    a plane *corkscrewing*

down into the verdant green
      neck of Baghdad's bottle-glass night
so I don't yet register the casual solemnity
    of newscaster banter

falling like spent shells
      from both our mouths, nor am I
startled by the feigned evenness
    in my lover's tone, the way

he wrests the brief quaver
      from his voice like a pilot

pulling hard out of an engineless
    plummet, but only at the last minute

    and with the cratered ground
        terrifying, in sight—

Notes on Atrocity (Baghdad Aid Station)

Mid-conversation someone comes
looking for body bags. Medic,

I can hear you rummaging
the shelves, know the small fury

of your hands and the way
they used to settle, palms sinking

heavy bodies into mine. Outside
on my end, frost whittles the grass

to shards, the pear tree breathes
beneath a shroud of ice. When your voice

drifts above the shifted boxes, overheard,
it's washed in a tenderness I know

I'm not supposed to hear. As if
this were not the work of shrapnel—

not the body's wet rending, flesh
reduced to matter—but the litany

of an old field guide, the names
of wildflowers spoken out loud:

ischium, basal ganglia, myelin-
sheathed endings. Names for parts.

For all our flowering parts.

After the Blast

It happened again just now. One word
snagging like fabric on a barbed fence.

Concertina wire. You said: *I didn't see the body
hung on concertina wire.* This was after the blast.

After you stood in the divot, both feet
in the dust's new mouth and found no one alive.

Just out of the shower, I imagine
a flake of soap crusting your dark jaw, the phone

a cradle for your bare cheek.
I should say: *love.* I should say: *go on.*

But I'm stuck on *concertina*—
the accordion's deep inner coils, bellows,

lungful of air contracting like a body caught
in the agony of climax. Graceless

before the ballooning rush
of air or sound. That battering release.

Aubade, Iraq

Sulfur-mouthed nightcrier, rooftop
harbinger, bringer of the gut-shot

dawn—what I would do to keep you
at rifle's reach, stifle you, drown you

in the Tigris' muck and swill, touch you
aflame on its kerosene spine.

I could wait out artillery skitter, crater-
blast, stay here long into next empire

dreaming fingers and the Fertile Crescent
of thighs—if not for your voice

risen like Babel's ghost from the ruined fortress,
ash-haired rider come to tongue open

dawn's torturous eye—

The Riots in Bangalore

*An icon of South Indian cinema and star of more than 200 films,
Raj Kumar died on Wednesday, sparking widespread violence as
distraught fans torched buses and ripped scaffolding in the country's
hi-tech hub.*—REUTERS

Morning in April, the war still on, sun silting the kitchen
like coffee grounds in the sink. In yesterday's *Times*

mourners in India ripped doors from hinges, smashed

loose shutters. Like the ancient Rites of Spring—
steer roasts in the budding groves, lions waiting to be fed—

the pageantry of death so close to bliss. The street's all aftermath:

torched cars, trampled grass. The day hoisted by its shoulders
and carried away. After all these months, I've come to expect

nothing less of despair. A hero dies and why not

take to the streets, join the cherry trees rallying into bloom?
Death so close you can reach out and tear a board

from the casket, taste the bitter singe of rubber in the air.

And why not follow the ambulance like Orpheus's keening
head down the river of bodies, add another voice to the severed

song? Even now, as grief threatens to strip the world to its naked

scaffolding—the war entering a third year, you still nine months
from home—blossoms swarm my window and the sun

impulsively flashes, bare flesh beneath a shredded veil.

The First Canto

I know you've waited for this call all day, felt the tank's
panes rattle twice from the nearest shell, air shuddering

like talus underfoot. Ninety-eight degrees in Baghdad
and you say the heat hasn't yet arrived, though I can feel it, the armored

weight of days, your voice spreading like crescents of sweat
beneath each fold of cloth. Today I don't ask about the war, your afternoon

shredding envelopes into the burn barrel, if any bodies came in.
Instead, I want to tell you about the First Canto, dark woods, a trail

turned first to thicket and then to shale. A man brought to the edge
of the cindery lip to peer in. Even Dante had a choice: to ascend

the sunny mantle of light or take the fast slope down, to flee
the wolf approaching, his own fear. There was no catch

but the cold lake growing in his heart, small terror
like the plash of an oar loosened from its hold. He didn't wait

to see the wolf's gray mange, its scurvied hide, the broken teeth
betraying hunger for the sun. He chose first to descend, and you—

you chose the war. Seventeen months now and you're a shade
leaning into the soot-grimed mouth of the oil drum, whip of sparks

lashing your hands, the book I sent you, unread, at your feet.

The War Bride Waits

Sometimes it's like the last scene in a Western where only the horses are left
grazing an apocalypsed field. There they are, stranded amid crabgrass in the
    blessing

of their own bulky bodies, having survived the long ride, having missed
the bullets of outlaws or the tragic implications of fate, quietly bathed in a gold
    light

meant to signify the dawning END. There's always a fade-out, the rising
bird-on-a-bent-wing scrawl of names meaning we should expect nothing more,

no last plot twist, no surprise rock-fall, no lover waiting off-screen to turn up
for the hero's dream of death. This is the moment the dead are mercifully
    allowed

to stay dead, the moment in the dull celluloid flicker when the last horse caught
in the narrowing lens lifts its bent neck expectantly and looks around.

Planting, Hayhurst Farm

A week since the last bombing
brought you to your knees, since

the day you spent shoveling
human remains into a body bag

marked for home. I don't know
what to say. Neither of us has slept.

But today, planting peppers
on a farm in Oregon nowhere near

the war, I found myself mid-way
down a row, on all fours, hands

breaking open the rocky clods
coaxing the flimsy necks to stand.

It felt like an exercise
in good faith—my fingers

blindly plunging, a brief tenderness
exacted on every stalk.

Some didn't make it through
our rough caging, some will never

bear fruit. I don't know if this
is even meant as consolation

but I want to tell you just how easy
it became to plant the thin bodies

in the ground, to mound up
the dense soil and move on.

Love in Wartime (II)

Outside, on the rocks
      the Japanese maples thrash
            their wind-wracked limbs.

The clamor of branches, lines
      of worshippers stampeding a mosque;

your gloved soldier's hands feeding out
      bloodied reams of gauze.

                        Holy, holy, holy:

the violence of those leaves, their purple,
            arterial sheen.

I want to say
is what I keep saying, over and again.

It goes on like this.

The wind, the saying, the not—

Public Mourning (Flag Installation)

One-hundred-sixty-six thousand flags
sodding the lawn like the hand-flung crumple
of scrap on the Liberation Day street. Ticker-
taped. Wired down into unfreeze, ground-
swell, into a harvest of heave and worm.

One-hundred-sixty-six thousand paper
carapaces like the eyelids of the living
sprung forth with all the nubbled blindness
of the newly dead. O make of me a human
camera to translate this restless flock.

Friendly Fire

i.

Caught between gunner and gunner,
slough and sand bank, clamor and clamor.

                              Pill and bitter pill.

ii.

Also called *fratricide*. As if
uniforms or tanks made kin, brothered-in-

        Cain rising from dune-heather
                like tracer smoke, ultimatum.

        Abel tripping through the seam-rent dawn
                into the eye of the scope.

Above the thornbelt, sky'd shrapnel, God's own eyes
                        waiting to see what would be done.

iii.

        As if the flames were meant alone to warm.

        Cookfire, hearth, hot rocks for bread.
                The lit faces of ecstatics. A joyful flickering.

iv.

Slender-tongued tracer arc. Sweet talker.

Long-time lover throwing wide her arms
to shield you. Friendly fire, sulfur-choked

passion—nothing of betrayal sparking
her open and tendered mouth.

Metal Sandwich

In the dream-logic of last night's two separate dreams
I ate metal in a doughy bun and then watched my molars
crumble and split lengthwise in the next. *Rotten junk,*
the dream doctor said and tendered a metal fist before
I woke to a morning full of consequence and holes.

Ballistic

The article quoted the private as saying
they'd been *thinking with their guns again*

by way of explanation. The context doesn't matter;
the soldiers were expected to survive. It's not hard

to imagine the brain's ballistics, tamped neurons,

a bullet throttled from bore to breech. Take the way
I understood last night's dream. One crumbling tooth

as the ghost pain of a limb my body had become—
and then you gone when I dreamed I woke and gone still

for the real waking, morning's paralysis of sun.

What strange misfire, stutter in the synaptic gap,
though it could be much worse: all coordinates

misaligned or lost, the real bullet fished finally
from the unconscious sergeant's skull

and strung around his waiting lover's neck.

For L., in Baghdad

A fuselage of crows beggars
the January seed. They lurch from limbs

then upstart, near the ground. Iron marrow,
rust. What happened to the will to fly?

Here, it's record-breaking cold. A breaking
cold that never breaks.

Do me a favor, L. Stay put. Stay close
to earth. The days are nose-diving

to an end. Keep a record of the bodies there
and I will keep a tally here of mine.

Refusing Beatrice

Dante needed a whole committee—
Beatrice, Lucy, Virgil—to guide him

      down and back, even though hell

was a known descent, a matter of pages, a book
ending in certainty with a hero seeing stars.

   You've got no itinerary. Just an armored car
     to ferry you down the graveled airport road, a Chinook

     gut-deep in the green swill waiting to dislodge.

Maybe it's time to stop comparing—
I could never be Beatrice, couldn't harbor such good faith.

   And I won't be there in the Tigris basin to watch
     heat flake cinders of paint from the Chinook's body
        like a rug shook out

  or see it hasten to the sky's surface
      like an untethered corpse—

My curse or gift is blindness;
    I've never read this story before.

   And if the updraft's whirlwind
     doesn't make the sniper miss, if your helicopter lifts

from Baghdad as doomed as the Chaldean sun,

I won't be there to see the wreckage

or papery flames, the falling arsenal of stars—

Love in Wartime (III)

The teacher wanted a clearer starting place.

A map or else a mapping on.
Towns, green hills, a common vein of road.

Newspapers that spoke overtly
or else never spoke of war.

But in the poem's road
there was always something burning.

Petrol blue-smoked the borders
and no one was allowed out or in.

Somewhere a clot of tarmac singed
brightly like light through scrubby trees

and it was impossible to step from the median
without mouthing
                    minefield, lodestar, beautiful amputee—

Charon

Before the Acheron, before the fret and fester
of oars in the stream, before days that mounted
like carcasses stripped from shades and the words
for everything sloughed like side-meat
from water-softened bone—

There was *sun* and *slough*.
There was *shin-deep in the quick waters*
and places where the mayflies' wing-drag
filigreed the air, where my own hook-flash
wracked the mud-skinned surface

and a hundred violent mouths rose up to feed.

For Radha, Two Days Old

It's winter and the war's still on.

Ice cauls our windows. Snow
paraffins the trees.

No silage, no petrol, no forethought
can save us from this cold,

nor spring return to us
our dead.

Just days ago, slash smoldered
along the coast road.

Hold on, tiny faith, warm coal.
Radha, let us touch your face,

thaw our fingers on your kindled skull,
trace the kerf of your open mouth.

Abide us.

The fields are stubble
where the drip-torch slurred.

We have nothing left to burn.

Aftermath

        His job was not to salvage
but to bundle the clothes—trash bags full of uniforms
Rorschached in blood, boot-tips testing toed-thin plastic
like cheekbones testing skin, loose tongues in search
of a foot or a name—
                    and then carry it all out
to the incinerator and wait until new smoke hoisted
        the black flag of daybreak that would billow and rise and fade.

Late February (Persephone)

In the front yard I loosen sod,
return the lawn to earth and seed,
listen for the twang of the spade-head
channeling the chthonic ground.

Meanwhile the earth stands still.
The sun's ball bearing cools, gaskets
out of time and in the limbs of trees
the water-thinned sap unspools.

This month extends its promise of rain and rain-
greased boughs but instead of amends I make
myself a bulb in a worm hole, mouth piece
for the spade-mouthed dead.

What We Hold, We Hold at Bay

Along the hedge along the rail
lilacs hold purple bouquets of rain

at eye-level, leveling the dewy
buckets of their eyes at mine

so passing the next flower-mortared
wall I swipe a slice of leaf and press

its lacquered numerals to my wrist
to let its oaky face-plate register my pulse.

Palm Reader, I read a patchy guess-
work and hold the leaf the way

I think you must have held
a dog tag slipped from around the collar

of the dead before you zipped the soldier
into his leafy cask—

                     but I can't decipher a name

from any of these veins or read
the engrafted petals of this Braille

and without a chain to save it on
I can only lift it to the record of my lips:

leaf-metal burnished with the breath
of rain, on which I try to find your breath—

Clamor

Staking fencing along the border of the spring

garden I want suddenly to say something about

this word that means sound and soundlessness

at once. The deafening metal of my hammer strikes

wood, a tuning fork tuning my ears to a register

I'm too deaf to understand. Across the yard

each petal dithers from the far pear one white

cheek at a time like one blade of snow into

the next until the yard looks like the sound

of a television screen tuned last night to late-

night static. White as a page or a field where

I often go to find the promise of evidence of you

or your unit's safe return. But instead of foot-

prints in the frosted static there's only late-

turned-early news and the newest image of a war

that can't be finished or won. And because last

night I turned away from the television's promise

of you I'm still away. I've staked myself

deep to the unrung ground, hammer humming

in my hand, the screen's aborted stop-time still

turning over in my head: a white twist of rag

pinned in the bloody center of a civilian's chest,

a sign we know just enough to know it means

surrender, there in the place a falling petal's heart would be.

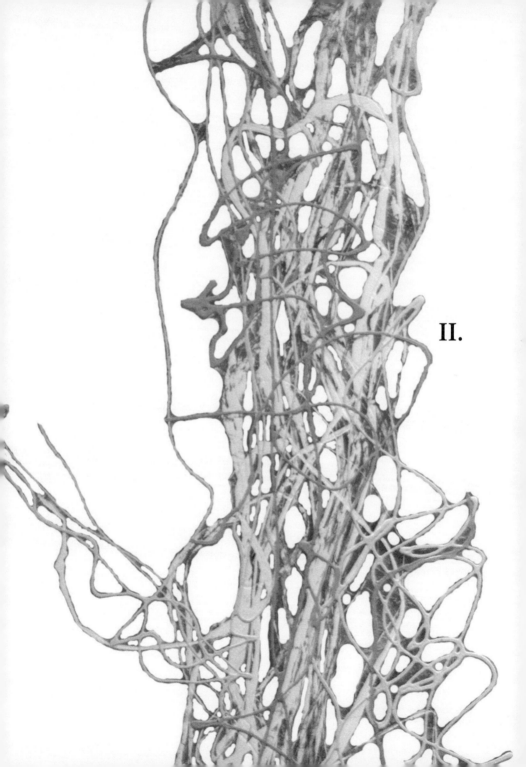

II.

shift of form &
pov

Deployment Ends

November morning. Dusky pellicle of frost on the ground. When his plane
finally touched down, when he imagined her pocketed hands, her pacing in the
terminal, he thought he would have to turn away. There was too much harm
in the world for this small province of safety to go acknowledged. When he
walked down the long terminal he swung his hands. As if he had no baggage
to remind him of the way.

After the War

They lived like revenants, just outside the gate. He was The Returned. She was the one who propped the storm door to watch the empty street. The first lesson was simple: learn the name of a blessing and then speak it within earshot of the other. At first she could only think, *Meekness*. January's thigh-shriveled light or the muteness, even, of birds. The way a whole tree's-worth of crows enacted Quiet-Homage-to-Despair and not one of them ever startled at the Apaches throttling overhead.

At some point she forgot to think of a blessing. Even the days started to pass. And then this morning when she was standing in the doorway she saw the sun throw its jacket across the top of the barbed perimeter fence—like an escapee—so that nothing would catch or tear. The next blessing would have to be forgiveness and for a whole day she believed it would last.

By Omission

I didn't know I was empty-holstered, her husband was saying, *until after we'd passed the gate.* They were at the kitchen table with the neighbors and everyone but her was back from war. The light outside was dusk, a rag full of holes, an hourglass leaking salt. A neighbor flipped a bottle cap in his hand. She'd heard about the bodies, his bagging of the dead, how to pull a dog tag from its chain. But not this detail before. *How do you forget your gun?* she asked. She was imagining the empty cradle where he must have put his hand. Tenderness or refusal, thoughtlessness, surprise or dread. Outside, the dusk was losing. A glass sang out against the table's edge and when he said nothing she knew every silence was a lie he couldn't tell.

Commerce

There wasn't enough forgiveness to go around. Dogs led themselves around the block. At the pawn shop down the street you could buy anything, even someone else's false teeth. The whole day it rained and then was sunny and then it rained some more. She was sitting at her desk reading a book. When she looked a word up in the dictionary, she remembered one from a dream. It was just like that, two for the price of one, and then, action following word: how she pulled the plug from the wall and *wound* the cable up; how when he came back into the room in his uniform, the *wound* opened some more. Each meaning haunted by the next. By then it was growing dark and the whole western sky was gold pried from a stranger's mouth. There are smaller prices for having survived.

Complicity

She's halfway through the line at the store when she overhears the clerk say, *My husband? He's off at war.* The clerk leans both hands on the counter like an old grandmother in some country of ground-freeze and broken glass. At the register they're two women across a plastic counter. Do they want to tell each other everything they know about the war? Some complicities she's never felt. In the other country, women gum seeds in their mouths, let the empty shells speak for themselves. On the counter, the paper receipt curls against itself. She reaches for spilled coins and feels a tongue push back against her teeth.

Endurance

I used to stand in doorways and know
there was no human way to go on or through—

Mercy

I had a friend who broke his neck in a rugby game. One straight fracture right at the base, only he didn't know it and neither did we. He went home that night in pain and didn't come out to the bar. When we called the next morning he'd already driven himself to the hospital where they'd guided him into a C-collar and bolted a metal halo to his skull.

I remembered him just now when I ran my hand along your scalp, the divot where a surgeon's scalpel dove. Even before you left for war, you had these scars to show. Bone fused just at the brink. I think I envy your surgeon his hands, the deftness of a bone-saw sunk from skull to blade guard, their knowledge that mercy's sole attendant is pain.

I don't believe in any higher power, my friend was saying the time I saw him next. *But if I had had to turn my head at any point along the way, I would be dead.* For every word he spoke, the halo's shadow trembled, lightening his darkened face.

Bridge

One fall we humped logs up to a bridge site near Wildcat, bushwhacked a shortcut the entire way. Each time we dropped lumber at the site we pried up bridge spikes and shouldered chunks of the rotten stringers for the trip down. For three days it went on like that, shouldering and un-shouldering loads, mashing ferns into duff, tearing briars and their rusty cables from our hair. Late October and the season was about to unleash a killing cold. Our work was supposed to be done. We beat the snow until the new bridge had to go up. I remember nothing of that process. Only flakes beginning to thicken on our last trip down, that final, stricken weightlessness like submission or the moment I realized you'd survived the war though the war would never be won.

Married

In a backyard tent I told you the story of Guy Waterman's ghost. How, climbing past Little Haystack, the wind took up the dirt into his form and then was gone. There was the sound of rockslide but not a single stone had moved. You told me about a child who pressed herself into the attic window while the rest of her body burned. On the upper lining of our tent was a skin of breath or early dew. And after making love, we made of our returning bodies a smoky pane so that the dead could see us too.

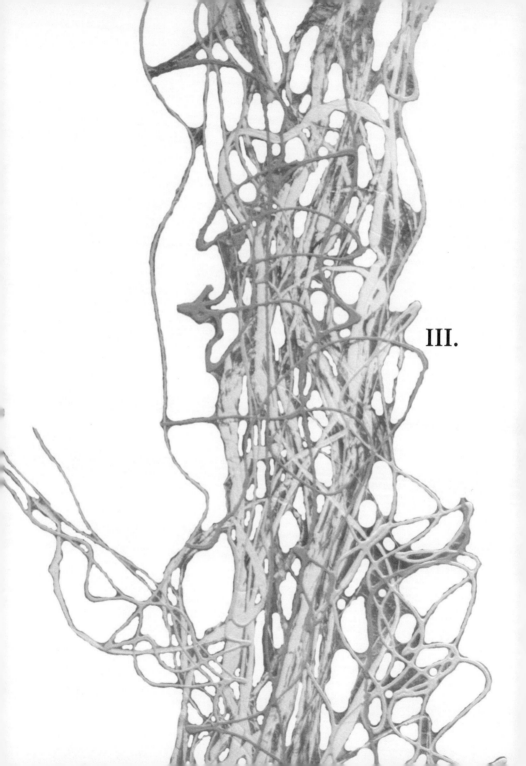

III.

Through a round aperture I saw appear
Some of the beautiful things that Heaven bears,
Where we came forth, and once more saw the stars.

INFERNO, CANTO XXXIV

Veteran's Day

Today the wind's predictable, flowering the brown lawn
with the dead gloved thumbs of leaves like a rusted

poppy-strafed field.   *Live Oak*

I remember hearing for the first time long before Texas—
without knowing taxonomy or that living

basketry of limbs—and thinking in what desolate
place is this title not redundant?

Live Oak, quercus virginiana. And now I see it's a name
befitting itself and I want to rename everything this morning:

Live Low Cumulus   Live Rain-Sheened Street   Live Sun

bone-sawing through a gap in the leaves. And earlier, Live
Flesh of your flesh when I slipped my hand beneath your shirt

and felt the impatient work of your working heart
from beneath an unwreathed cenotaph. Your ribs.

Mesquite

All I want above my grave is a mesquite tree
   Frank Dobie said, so all morning on your stoop

outside the base's barbed perimeter fence, I've been reading
   mesquite as testament to readiness

and thirst, leaves chittering above hardpan and roots
   displacing everything that came before.

What memorial: sweet starch of survival
   in the bark, needles re-threading the shaggy limbs.

And now, asleep on the couch in your desert
   camo, boot tips splayed like dead cactus flowers,

your body's a spiny thorn and there are shovel-blunt
   consequences for your return. Alkaline veins

in the earth, raptors stealing sun or the metal
   husks of shells and no chance

for a quick or catastrophic death. Sleep, my love,
   my Hopeless Returned. Leaf out

into another body: the body no waking moment
   will allow you to become—

Persephone as Model for the Soldier, Returned

Imagine villagers outside Avernus leaving
their stoves ajar, tongues guttering the grates,

to see what flame you'd remake your body by.

Spring, and with a villager's hands I crack
black rot from shells, hedge old bets and push the beans

down into unfreezing muck. Re-read
the almanac's advice on how to overwinter well

and wait.

*

Waiting, I watched forsythia come alive
between the fence's broken slats.

And when I looked up, a bottle rolled, wind-
gust down the street.

Was it like that?

Simply obeying a season?
February's slow-becoming Spring?

*

Beneath the Spring, tectonic plates that never
quit. A voice saying *Don't forget!* even as

it was starting to break up.
On the surface, snow's crackle, static.

A puddle of grackles beak-deep in mud.
One long tremor after another

and the birds still jawing and diving
as if trying to get through.

*

Even as we made it through, planting
seeds in earthen pots, in rows, in

the overbearing ground, we took
your silence for the slow speech of thaw.

How could we have known a pit
stuck like a bloody molar in your mouth?

The thing that, trying and trying,
                    you can never spit out—

*

Split root, dual stranger. Beloved.

Please tell me only your feet remember
what the earth beneath the earth was like.

Your Plane Arrives from Iraq for the Last Time

Texas overcast. The road toward post
needle-pricked in brake lights, start-
and-stop of the heart's four chambers

involuntarily bound. And once more
the sky's feathered jet-stream, and once
more, the dirge and caesura of rotors

and once more the slow Morse of the plane's
body descending. And at the end
of the longest sentence I've ever known

your face in the window's fogged aperture:
stranded noun, Rorschach of stars. *Beautiful thing.*

Garden

No gardener, you watch from the deck
as I scrape weedy belts from the green
waists of spinach and kale. May evening

and the sun's bayoneted on a paintless post
across the yard—enough to blind us with—
so when I look up from the slaty loam I look

East and catch you squinting into the ambered
blood of the Western sky, a glassy shoot of bottle-
light sprouted from your Returning Soldier's hands.

After Discussing Your Original Reasons for Enlisting

I dream we're raccoon traders hustling punctuation-
sized babykins out of their thatch-box rookeries—they're
more like chickens in the cellular dreamlight—and our BB
guns are smokeless invocations. When the cops come at full
tilt in a golf cart I can only stand and gawk at the questions
forming in the question-riddled air while you, my heartthrob
war hero minus the hero, stand mute as a comma, one insistent
newborn mewling in the crook of each hesitant arm.

Poem Without Throat or Song

Morning finds me over-
steeped   a garden unturned

unshirred clod thieved
from frost's last catacomb

a dew-wrecked coffer   a dormant
lantern   a muted cocoon

a guttering guildering

a guilting thing—

Conversation

We're disparate as men counting
miles across an ocean renamed home,
you and I and the heart's joists that keep
the roof from warping under broken

pipes and wind. *No one marries during war,*
I'm told and yet I'm married to the thought
of you returning home to marry me
to my former self. The war is everywhere

at once. Each eggplant that I pick
is ripe and sun-dark in its own inviolable
skin. Except there is no inviolable anything
and you've been home now for a year.

In the Fourth Year of War (Killeen, TX)

Here, morning means another
dogged black wing of light snagged

like a wind-gust bag plastered
to the perimeter fence;

you gone before crow-squawk wakes
the standing legion of trees.

What the trees forgive I have
tried as well: dawn's doilied prayer

scarf lifted from their armored
limbs before any prayer's

been said; or the hasped voices
of crows, their rotor-edged nay-

saying like the constant drone
of planes. *Come back O Come Back.*

Every morning test flights test
my old resolve to stay close

to earth. Call it failure or
respite, call it gravity's

portrait of grace. Still, there's no
disputing the stuttered flight

of light or crows from one branch
to the gnarled next. They lift

and drop and snag like notes
along the heart's barbed chord. A song.

Commission

In the poem you asked me for we're driving
West—though we never have before—toward
the western sun and each mile gained we slough

a bit of self. By the time we hit the coastal
shacks we're cliff-side and eroded bare. Or else
eroded new. With what measured mercy I can proffer

you I draw a fishing boat's fresh clutch of gulls
to swoon in circles overhead and hinge my hands
into the razor clam's promise of sand or sandy flesh.

North Coast

I.

All evening the best-of-the-season sun's been faking
resurrection, wandering an astral boast above our sun-

burnt heads while we probe the shore's supply
of tide-worn stones for surface travel on a glazier's bay.

Low tide unscrolls a surfy bricolage of shell
and carapace and kelp and finally we're prepared to see

whatever else we stand to lose. Civilian at last
you squint into the dazzling proof of sun, warm stone

in your stone-warmed hands and say, *I've never seen a day
last through itself like this*, then stand and chuck the stone
                                        into the seamless bay.

II.

The sea lifts its mapmaker's hands
to the silty bay edge, drafting a border
in briny scrawls the squirts and crabs

ignore. This close to North the sun
protracts an angle heretofore unknown

as all things I didn't know before
you returned from war. Now

you drowse across a splintered sea-
drift log, arms loosened at their sockets
like the unbuckled carapace of crab

beaked belly-up by a marauding gull:
that winning Portrait of a Fallen Hero pose.

Near sleep too, I build a driftwood
raft with woody rays of sun to drift us

out past tide break so that I might shoot
a bull-kelp bearing in sixty-four directions
and sketch out the farthest skein of map

the tide's—just now—withdrawn.

The Dreams

O The Dreams are back, The Dreams won't let me
        alone, The Dreams have gatekeepers
in trench coats woven from tire shavings and thorn

and whenever I hasten toward the sleep of the sleep-
        bludgeoned, the boulder placid in a talus-field of sleep
the gatekeepers shake the rattlesnake bushes that pillow

my head and club the cracked parchment of my feet.
        O The Dreams are bitter, are creosote and char and can't
let me forget their dozen names. The Dream of Death or Dis-

appointment, the Dream of the Inscrutable with its hot
        disks tattooed like your name into flesh, stripped
guy-lines to hoist the crow-sorrowed horizon aloft.

Coffee

Because the brew I'm steeping sees me mid-page
through a book of poems about the war I have to
choose whether to leave this page's body for grinds
that burble through the coffee press like the body
of the early-winter earth that called me to attention
with its empty-handed mix of mud and snow the day
I deemed you *Morning Wisp of Dew* zeroing like steam
from the top of my daily mug—or else sit through
these kettle-thralls until they wake you from the war
into our room nearby where the sheets are pages
I've torn back in search of morning's grinds, and you.

Days and Nights of Your Return

Sometimes it's darkness the heart's engine
lifts the body into. Like the test flights

of aircraft crowning the night's steady tar

or thought's crook-necked bird nestled
unspoken in the brain's loose scree.

As if there were something preternatural

about the rise of any form into a visible
space—the blind whir of rotors

bearing the plane's body into foggy view

or the acetylene shock of the skin's
presence becoming known—

From a separate darkness we number

the days, watch our bodies' stricken falling
from a distance, each feather of longing

skiffed off a turning wing.

Infidelity

When you were in Iraq I dreamed you
dead, dormant, shanked stone

in a winter well, verb-less object
sunk haft-deep through the navel

of each waking sentence. I dreamed
myself shipwreck, rent timbers

on a tidal bed, woke to morning's cold
mast of breath canted wide as a search light

for the drowned. Dreamed my crumbling
teeth bloomed shrapnel'd bone light

bricks mortared into a broken
kingdom of sleep where I found you

dream-sift, rubbled, nowhere.
Forgive me, love, this last

infidelity: I never dreamed you whole.

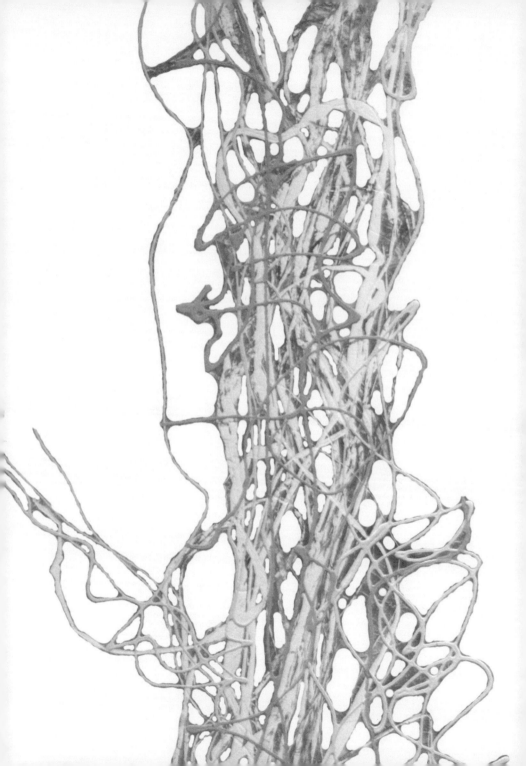

Roll Call

No matter the details. It always ends
at the sweat-salt metal of your un-
answered name. Twenty-one triggers
and twelve-hundred bit-down tongues.

Last clamor of the swan-beaked rifle.
Last unmuzzled throatful of air.